What Are Your Rights and Responsibilities?

UNDERSTANDING CITIZENSHIP

Rory McCallum

CIVICS FOR THE REAL WORLD™

Rosen Classroom™

Published in 2019 by The Rosen Publishing Group, Inc.
29 East 21st Street, New York, NY 10010

Book Design: Haley Robinson
Editor: Ryan Wolf

Photo Credits: Cover wavebreakmedia/Shutterstock.com; p. 4 michaeljung/Shutterstock.com; p. 7 Charles Brutlag/Shutterstock.com; p. 8 Cory Seamer/Shutterstock.com; p. 11 CRAZYBOM/Shutterstock.com; p. 12 Alexandru Nika/Shutterstock.com; p. 14 Dmytro Zinkevych/Shutterstock.com.

ISBN: 9781538365410
6-pack ISBN: 9781538365427

Manufactured in the United States of America

CPSIA Compliance Information: Batch #WS18RC: For Further Information contact Rosen Publishing, New York, New York at 1-800-237-9932

Table of Contents

Freedoms and Duties

As a citizen of the United States, you have some important rights. You also have responsibilities, which are duties you are expected or required to do. You might think that only adults have these rights and responsibilities, but that's not true. You have rights, and there's a lot you can do to be a responsible citizen!

The Bill of Rights

The most important rights that U.S. citizens have are promised to them by the Bill of Rights. The Bill of Rights includes the first ten amendments, or changes, to the U.S. **Constitution**. These rights include freedom of speech. The First Amendment says people have the right to say what they want to without being controlled or **punished** by the government.

Bill of Rights

HUMAN RIGHTS
It's Girls Like Me
who will one day
CHANGE THE WORLD

Even More Rights

People also have the right to **assemble** peacefully. They can meet to talk or **protest** things the government does. They can petition, or ask, the government to fix something that's wrong. Citizens are also promised the right to a fair **trial**. There are more rights, too. The Bill of Rights even states that there are more rights than the ones the Constitution includes.

Responsible

With these rights, however, there are responsibilities. Citizens need to obey the laws. They should make sure the laws are fair. All citizens can work to make sure the country runs the way it should. They have the responsibility to do things to benefit their community, their country, and their fellow citizens. They can use their rights to do this!

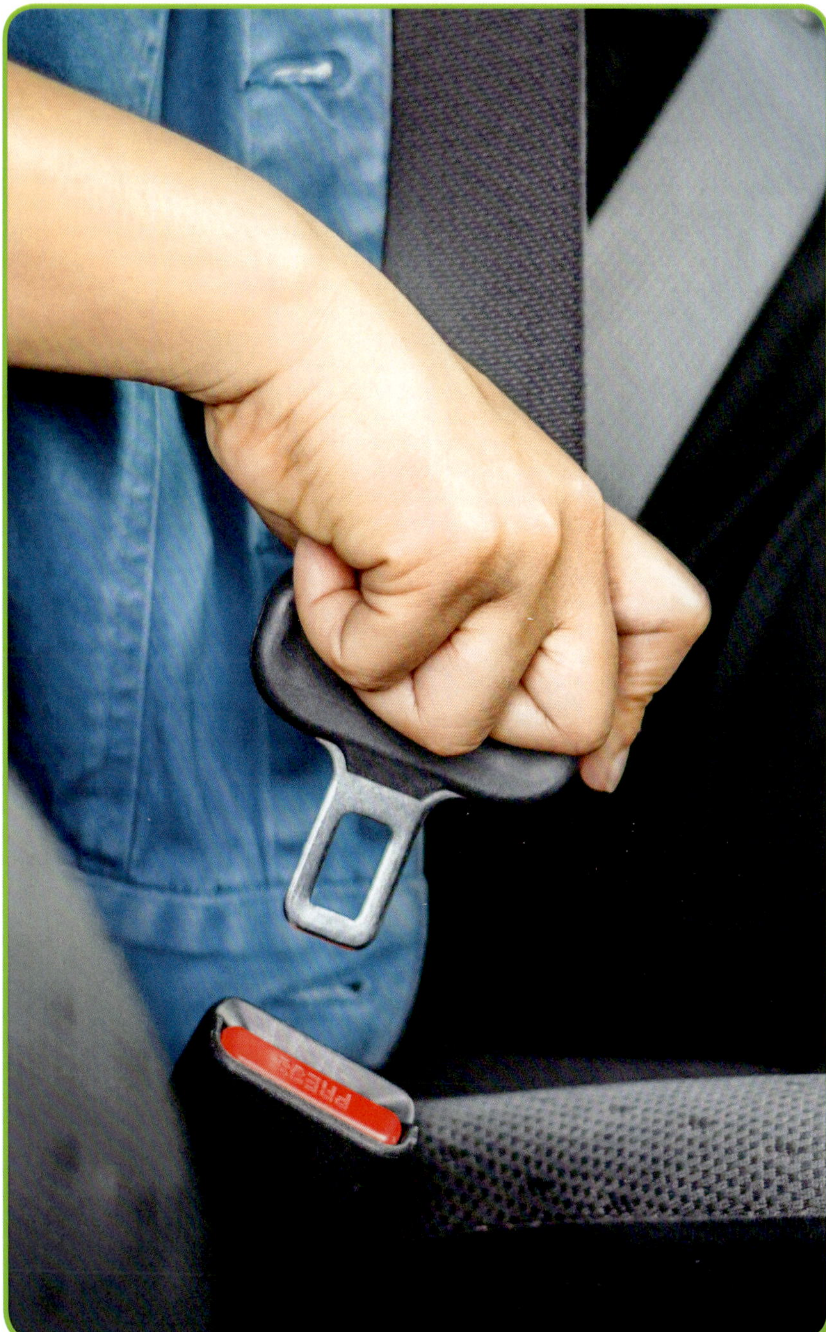
PRESS

The Power of Voting

One of the biggest responsibilities that adults have is to vote. This is also one of their most important rights! People can vote for leaders they think will lead the country or their community in a good way. They can vote for laws they think will help people. It's very important to vote. If you don't vote, you don't have a say in the government.

A Super Citizen!

You might not be able to vote yet, but you do have rights and responsibilities. You can be a responsible citizen by working for the common good of your community. This means that you do things that benefit your community. You can follow laws and rules. You can also make sure you treat your fellow citizens well and respect their rights, too!

Glossary

assemble: To meet together in one place.

constitution: The basic laws by which a country, state, or group is governed.

protest: To show or state strong disagreement with or disapproval of something.

punish: To make someone suffer for something he or she has done.

trial: A meeting in a court in which lawyers, or people who help other people with the law, present information for a decision about a law case.

Index